Lisa Saavedra's

GOLF
ETIQUETTE
FORE YOU

with
Cruz Saavedra

Illustrated by Kimmberly A. Ioane-Venezio

7TH AVENUE PUBLISHING
San Jose, California

Publisher's Cataloging-In-Publication Data
Saavedra, Lisa S.   Golf Etiquette Fore You

ISBN 1-881931-49-8
Library of Congress Catalog Card Number:
92-61539

7TH AVENUE PUBLISHING
P.O. Box 24552
San Jose, CA 95154

Printed in the United States of America

Copy Editor - Debra H. Woods

Illustrations and cover design -
Kimmberly A. Ioane-Venezio

DEDICATED TO ALL
WHO HAVE CHOSEN TO PLAY
THIS INCREDIBLE, INTRIGUING
AND ABSORBING SPORT.

GOLF ETIQUETTE FORE YOU is a simple tool to help you polish your golfing "finish".

This book with enjoyable illustrations and a "picture is worth a thousand words" style will benefit your learning wisdom. Along with common sense, a helpful mentor, and lots of experience on the course contribute to a golfer's knowledge and application of the codes of courtesy. For a faster, fuller and more enjoyable game, read this book and set a good example.

ACKNOWLEDGEMENTS

This book was completed with the help of many people. Thank you for your time and energy.

Ernie Barbour, P.G.A.
Chris Burkhart, L.P.G.A.
Diane Daugherty, L.P.G.A.
Bob Fagan, N.C.P.G.A. Executive Director
Amy Geithner, L.P.G.A.
Brian Inkster, P.G.A.
Ken Klupa, Deep Cliff Golf Course
Jim Langley, P.G.A.
Shawn McEntee, P.G.A.
Larry O'Leary, P.G.A.
DeDe Owens, L.P.G.A.
Cheryl Pastore, L.P.G.A.
Jay Risso
Judee Risso
Kimberly Sandman, L.P.G.A.
Jackie Steinmann, L.P.G.A.
Keith Tatsuta
Roger Val, N.C.G.A.
Linda Vollstedt, L.P.G.A.
Kathy Wake, P.G.A./L.P.G.A.

Also Paul Lane, P.G.A., who wrote *Fast Play Keys* and has given his permission to reprint.

CONTENTS

WHY ETIQUETTE

The making of a successful golfer is not limited to skill. Certain behavior is expected of an experienced golfer. It is your responsibility to know the courtesies that players extend to each other. Knowledgeable players who employ the finer courtesies of golf not only set the example for good play, they are better prepared for a well paced game. They enjoy golf to its fullest and help others do the same.

Remember the golden rule, "Do unto others as you would have others do unto you." Experienced golfers are very supportive and understanding of those learning to play the game. They look forward to seeing you grow and develop as a golfer and playing partner. Always remember that the sophisticated player expects his or her playing partners to know the courtesies of the game and exhibit proper protocol. The player who acknowledges the codes of courtesy will be genuinely appreciated on the course.

AVOID SLOW PLAY

Due to the rise in popularity of the great sport of golf, the most looming problem on the course today is slow play. Slow play can be intolerable! It can sour the enjoyment of the game and greatly diminish concentration. It is important for everyone on the course to keep the play moving!

Again, it is your responsibility to learn how to keep a steady pace. It's clear to even the first time golfer, that excessive conversation will slow up play. Save that interesting conversation for the 19th hole. And know that as an inexperienced player, you are encouraged to pick up your ball and advance to the next hole if you are falling behind. The objective is to take care of yourself and your ball, and to keep up with the group ahead. Please familiarize yourself with the codes of courtesy and the Rules of Golf. As you continue to learn and play, golfing etiquette and proper pace will become second nature.

FAST PLAY KEYS

Waive Honors: Long ball hitters tee off last.

Be Ready: Play when safe to do so.

Don't Delay: Minimize practice swings.

Putt Continuously: Unless you will step on another's line.

Leave Green Area: A.S.A.P. Record scores after leaving.

Use Provisional Balls: For ball which may be lost or O.B.

WHERE TO PLAY
AS YOU LEARN

Visit a learning center (practice facility, driving range) to develop your skills.

Next, go to a 9 hole golf course to test and practice your new skills. The short course is a more comfortable and suitable place for the newcomer to relax and learn. Here you can incorporate the codes of courtesy and keeping pace skills into your game.

When you have more confidence and understand the courtesies that are expected of you, visit an 18 hole, par 3 course or play a 9 hole course twice. This will help you build your stamina and test your concentration. By the time you've learned your way around the course applying your course courtesy and keeping up with the group ahead skills, you'll be ready for the next step. Play a mid length course and finally graduate to a regulation course. Enjoy and Welcome!

GOLF CAR COURTESY

The courteous golf car driver generally rules in favor of common sense. However, here are a few important pointers to help keep up the pace of the game. Drive to the ball that is closest; the person whose ball is the furthest away can then drive to his or her ball when it is safe. The first golfer will then walk over to the car after executing his or her shot. If the golf ball of your partner flies in a different direction from yours, he or she should take a few clubs and walk to their ball. The driver will pick the other partner up. And lastly, each golf course has its own set of rules regarding motorized golf cars. Be aware of them!

GOLF
ETIQUETTE

BEING PREPARED

1. Each golfer must have a set of clubs.

2. Check into the pro shop at least 15 minutes prior to tee time.

3. When possible, play as a foursome. This speeds up the game.

13

4. Be able to identify your ball. Know the name and the number of the ball that you are playing. Mark your ball with a marker to identify it as yours.

5. Before teeing up, be prepared with the tools of the game — repair tool, ball marker, tees, extra balls, etiquette book and U.S.G.A. rule book.

17

6. Be aware of local rules. For instance, some courses do not allow rubber studded shoes and some have special car rules.

7. A round of golf should take a maximum of 4 to 4 1/2 hours. To maintain pace of play, stay within one half hole of the group ahead.

8. Stand still and be quiet when another golfer is addressing or hitting the ball.

9. Stay out of the peripheral vision of a golfer in the process of addressing or hitting the ball.

10. Wait to tee your ball until the previous golfer has completed his play.

11. Be sure the group
    ahead of you is out of
    range before hitting
    your ball.

12. Always yell an amplified "FORE" if your ball places others in danger.

31

13. No mulligans (second
     chances) allowed.

14. Park your golf carts in the direction of the next tee leaving a 15 foot distance from the putting surface and teeing area.

35

15. If you hear "FORE",
cover your head.

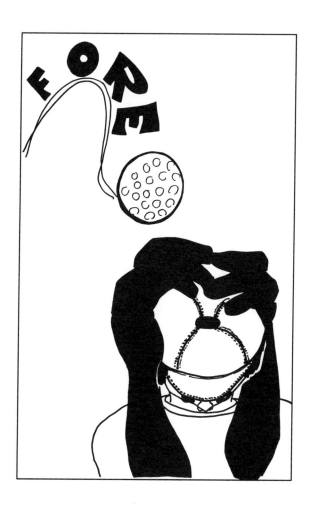

37

16. The player whose ball is farthest from green hits first. If your group is behind, hit when ready and safe.

17. One or two practice
     swings only please.

41

18. If safe, be up to your ball before your turn. You can stand off to the side then proceed when the player behind you finishes.

19. Make your club selection and assess yardage as you advance to your ball. This saves playing time.

45

20. Avoid lost balls by watching your ball, as well as your playing partner's ball, land, roll and stop. If it is far away, make note of a nearby landmark to make it easier to locate.

47

21. Play a provisional ball if you think that your ball may be lost or out of bounds.

49

22. All golfers in your group should assist in the search of a lost ball. A search for a lost ball should take no longer than five minutes. (This is also a golf rule!)

23. If your group is slow or play is delayed, let the players behind you play through.

53

24. When entering on to another player's fairway, players on that fairway have the right of way.

25. Replace your divots and those of others if time permits. Try to leave the course in better condition than you found it.

26. Rake the bunkers when you finish. Smooth over foot-prints and holes. Replace the rake in the bunker—teeth down.

ON THE GREEN

27. Place your golf bag
    carefully away from
    green.

61

28. Clean your spikes
while standing away
from tees and greens.

29. Walk carefully to avoid dragging your spikes or club on the green.

65

30. It only takes a player 5 seconds to repair a fresh ball mark; it will heal completely in 24 hours. A ball mark left unrepaired for 1 hour, takes 15 days to heal.

31. Clean the ball by rubbing it on a towel or on the rough around the green.

32. Be quiet and still on the green while the others are putting.

71

33. Read the green and prepare to putt while others are putting. Don't wait until it is your turn before you start the process.

34. Mark your ball on the green especially when it's in the line of another player or when it's in their view. When marking the ball on the green, place the marker behind the ball away from the hole.

35. Be careful not to step on another player's path to the hole.

36. If your marker inter-
feres with a player's
putting path, use your
putter head to mea-
sure. Move the marker
to one side in line with
a fixed object such as
a tree. Remember to
replace your marker
on the original spot.

37. The player whose ball is closest to the flagstick attends the flag after they have marked their ball. Stand away from the hole when tending to the flag or retrieving a ball.

38. The player farthest away from the hole on the green putts first.

39. Keep your shadow out of other golfers' putting paths.

40. Be gentle with the green and the hole, as they can be damaged easily. Retrieve the ball from the cup with your hand rather than your putter head. Be careful not to lean on the putter when taking the ball from the cup, as it can make a depression on the green.

41. When all players have holed out, the flagstick should be picked up and replaced with care to avoid denting the green or hole. The first golfer to hole out should be ready to replace the flagstick after everyone has putted.

42. Leave the green immediately after play; mark your score on the following tee.

91

MORE CONSIDERATIONS

43. "Honor" is when the player with the lowest score hits first. "Ready Golf", meaning the first person to be ready goes first, is often played because it speeds up the game.

93

44. Drive golf cars safely 30 feet away from bunkers, greens, and teeing areas. Stay on car paths unless otherwise posted.

95

45. Stash your trash in the provided receptacles.

TRASH CAN

46. Golf is a game of respect. Banging or throwing clubs can be hazardous.

47. Acknowledge the good play of others.

REMEMBER

PLEASE LEAVE THE COURSE IN BETTER CONDITION THAN YOU FOUND IT!

GLOSSARY

Ace	Hole-in-One
Address	Taking a stance that will enable you to make a golf shot.
Airmail	A golf shot which flies farther than anticipated and past the target.
Apron	Short grass (fringe) surrounding the putting green.
Away	The ball farthest from the hole. The away ball is played first.
Ball Mark	The depression on the green that a ball makes when it lands.
Ball Marker	A flat, small object used to mark the position of the ball on the putting surface. (e.g., a coin)
Banana Ball	A golf shot that curves excessively to the right for the right-handed person, or to the left for the left-handed person.
Birdie	One stroke under par.
Bogey	One stroke over par.

Breaking Putt	The curving path the ball takes due to gravity, grain and/or slope of the putting surface.
Bump and Run	A golf shot that is intentionally played into a bank or hill to lessen the speed, but continues to advance the ball forward.
Bunker	A hollowed area usually filled with sand. A sand trap is a type of hazard.
Buried Lie	A ball that is covered either by sand or grass.
Caddie	A person who assists a player by carrying clubs, helping with club selections, and providing information about the course such as terrain and distance to the flag.
Carry	The distance the ball travels in the air.
Casual Water	Temporary accumulation of water not intended to be a hazard, perhaps due to rain.

Chili Dip	To strike mother nature (earth) before the ball (fat shot); usually a pitch shot.
Chip Shot	A low trajectory shot played from close into the green which rolls farther than it flies.
Choke	A term used to describe FEAR!
Choke Down	To grip lower on the shaft of the club for more control.
Chunked Shot	See Fat Shot.
Cut Shot	A golf shot made with an open clubface while the clubhead path is moving to the left of the target. The ball will land softer with this shot.
Divot	Turf dug out by the club when making a swing.
Dog Leg	A golf hole that curves right or left.
Double Bogey	Two strokes over par.
Double Eagle	Three strokes under par.

Draw	A golf shot that curves mildly from right to left for the right-handed golfer, or left to right for the left-handed golfer; a small hook.
Driver	Club normally used to hit off the tee; #1 Wood
Duck Hook	A golf shot that curves sharply to the left for right handed-golfers, or to the right for left-handed golfers.
Eagle	Two strokes under par.
Explosion Shot	A golf shot made from a buried lie in a bunker.
Fade	A golf shot which curves moderately from left to right for the right-handed golfer, or right to left for the left-hand golfer.
Fairway	Closely mowed grassy area of play between tee and green.
Fairway Woods	#2 Wood, #3 Wood, #4 Wood, #5 Wood etc.

Fat Shot	A golf shot in which the club head hits turf before it hits the ball (Chunked Shot).
Flagstick	A moveable pole with a flag on top, placed in center of cup to mark the position of the cup. Also called the Pin.
Flier	A shot usually out of the rough that flies farther than expected.
Fore	A warning yell to any person in the path of the ball in play. (From the term 'forewarn', also from the use of 'forecaddies').
Fried Egg	A golf shot that lands in a sand bunker, splashes the sand, and stays in its own dugout.
Gimme	A putt that can't be missed (supposedly).
Golf Range	A practice facility.
Grain	The direction the grass grows on the putting surface.
Greenie	The ball on the green that is closest to the pin on a Par 3.

Ground	Touching the ground with the sole of the club while preparing for a shot.
Halved	When players score the same number on a hole, as in match play.
Handicap Index	A devised system to match the player's ability to that of the course. A system that makes the skill levels of the players equal so that they can compete fairly.
Hazard	A term used to identify bunkers or water areas. These areas will have yellow or red stakes around them.
Hole-in-One	Ball goes in the cup from the tee on the first shot on a par three hole. Also called 'Ace'.
Honor	The privilege to tee off first earned by having the lowest score on the preceding hole.
Hook	A golf shot that curves to the left for right-handed players and to the right for left-handed players.

Hosel	The part of the club that joins the clubhead to the shaft.
Irons	Irons are used to get the ball on the green or out of trouble. Short, Mid and Long Irons are used for greater accuracy.
L. P. G. A.	Ladies Professional Golf Association.
Lag	A long putt which is played intentionally short of the target so that it will stop close to the hole.
Lateral Water Hazard	Defined by red stakes—see hazard
Lay Up	A golf shot played intentionally short of the target.
Lie (Ball)	The position of the ball on the turf after it has come to rest.
Lie (Club)	The position that the sole of the club takes on the ground due to the angle of the shaft.
Line	The route the player chooses for the ball to travel toward the target.

Loft	The degree of slant which was designed into the clubface to raise the ball into the air and thus shorten the shot.
Long Irons	1,2,3 Irons.
Marker	The person who keeps score.
Match Play	Competition in which each hole is a separate contest. The winner is the one who wins the most holes.
Metal Wood	A club with a metal head used like a driver, 3 wood etc.
Mid Irons	4, 5, 6 Irons.
Mulligan	A takeover shot. Not sanctioned by the U.S.G.A.
Nassau	A golf bet which awards one point for the front nine, one for the back nine, and one for total round.
Oscar Brown	See Out of Bounds, O.B.

/

Out of Bounds	Also known as O.B. The area outside the boundaries of the golf hole you are playing. White stakes or fences mark the area. If the ball lands O.B., the shot is replayed with stroke and distance penalty.
P.G.A.	Professional Golf Association.
Par	The standard score designated for each hole of a golf course.
Pitch Shot	A high trajectory shot to the green that flies farther than it rolls.
Press	Doubling a bet, or to hit the ball harder than usual.
Provisional Ball	The second ball hit before the player looks for the first ball which is thought to be out of bounds or lost.
Pull Shot	A straight shot that flies to the left of the target area for a right-handed player or to the right for a left-handed player.

Punch Shot	A low trajectory shot executed by keeping the hands in front of the ball.
Push Shot	A straight shot which flies to the right of the target for the right-handed player and to the left for the left-handed player.
Quadruple Bogey	Four strokes over par.
Reading the Green	The attempt to judge the correct direction and distance to hole a putt.
Ready Golf	Whoever is ready, plays their ball. This speeds up the play. See 'Honor' for another way of playing.
Rough	Areas of uncut grass bordering the tee, fairway, hazards and green.
Sand Wedge	An extremely lofted club used in sand bunkers and close to the green.
Sandbagger	Charlatans who regularly score better than their handicap index.

Sandy	Making par from a sand bunker.
Shank	A golf shot hit off the hosel of the golf club.
Short Game	Refers to the shots played closest to and on the green with irons and putter.
Short Irons	7, 8, 9, wedge, sand wedge.
Skull	To strike the top of the ball causing a low shot.
Slice	A magnified fade.
Slope System	A calculated system which adjusts your handicap index at each course played.
Smother	To strike the ball with a closed clubface.
Stance	The position of feet at address.
Stroke	The forward motion of the clubhead with intent to strike the ball.
Stroke Play	A contest in which the total number of strokes is counted to win.

Stymied	An obstructed shot. Also known as 'in jail'.
Sweet Spot	The balanced position of the club face which does not impart torque when striking the ball.
Target Line	The line passing through the ball to the target.
Tee	A small peg on which the ball sits before striking it off the teeing area. The teeing area is also called the tee.
Tempo	The pace of the golf swing.
Timing	The numerical sequence of body and club movements used to perform the golf swing.
Topped Shot	To hit the ball above the center. Same as Skull.
Triple Bogey	Three strokes over par.
U. S. G.A.	United States Golf Association.
Unplayable Lie	A ball that the player considers unplayable.

Up and Down	Up on the green with a chip or pitch; down in the hole with one putt.
Waggle	Movements made for releasing tension before starting the golf swing.
Water Hazard	Defined by yellow stakes—see hazard
Wedge	An extremely lofted club for use around the green; allows the ball more air time than roll.
Whiff	A swing that completely misses the ball; counts as a stroke.
Worm Burner	A low golf shot or grounder.
Yips	A mental process which affects the nerves. Usually associated with putting but can also appear during other parts of the short game.

ABOUT THE AUTHOR

Lisa Saavedra is a regular contributor of articles focused on the game of golf. She has done extensive research on golf and golf etiquette. **GOLF ETIQUETTE FORE YOU** is the result of a year of dedicated research and writing.

Ms. Saavedra is a member of the Ladies Professional Golf Association and a successful golf instructor. She takes professional pride in helping each student play to their personal potential. "Just as there is no perfect swing, there are no perfect players…but we are getting closer." Her *Keep It Simple* clinics are extremely popular in the Santa Clara County community.

Lisa and her husband Cruz are dedicated to this great sport,and spend hours practicing what they teach.